Ask...

(Life's Most Important Answers Are Found in Asking the Right Questions)

by
John L. Mason

Tulsa, Oklahoma

Ask...
(Life's Most Important Answers Are Found in Asking the Right Questions)
ISBN 1-56292-299-8
Copyright © 1997 by John Mason
P. O. Box 54996
Tulsa, OK 74155

Published by Honor Books
P. O. Box 55388
Tulsa, Oklahoma 74155

Dedication

I am proud to dedicate this book to my beautiful wife, Linda, and our four great kids Michelle, Greg, Mike, and Dave.

To Linda, for being my very best friend.

To Michelle, "Moosh," for your love.

To Greg, "The Z," for your non-stop sense of humor.

To Mike, "Mister Mikey," for your inquisitiveness.

To Dave, "The Kumba Man," for your contagious smile.

Introduction

Over the past several years, I have had the privilege of knowing and working with many successful people from various walks of life. As I observed these people, I noticed that the "success traits" each possessed varied greatly from one individual to another. For example, some were very organized, whereas others seemed only to "file by pile." Although some worked long hours, weekends, and holidays, many could have written the book *How To Work a Four-Hour Day!*

One thing I learned for sure: There are a lot of ways to succeed. However, one common characteristic that is usually overlooked really stood out to me about these successful people: They all had the ability to ask good questions. In fact, many asked great questions on a regular basis.

I saw that whether or not these people who had attained success took action was greatly influenced by the questions they asked. I also observed that as they asked more outstanding questions, their focus in life changed and improved. They automatically became more productive! I began to realize that quality questions produce a quality life.

The Bible says, "Ask and you will receive" (Matthew 7:7) and "You have not because you ask not" (James 4:2). There is only one way to ask, and that is to pose a question! The way to receive is to ask questions.

That is why I wrote this book. I have collected a host of powerful questions that have impacted my life and the lives of others. These thought-provoking questions helped us find some of life's most important answers. I know they will do the same for you.

Remember, it's not only the questions you ask, but the questions you fail to ask, that shape your destiny. As you read this book, open your heart and mind. Let God whisper in your ear. Take action on the answers that come your way. Tap into the power of asking the right questions!

Looking Inward

Do you need a good

swift kick in the seat

of your <u>can'ts</u>?

Do you count your blessings, or do you think your blessings don't count?

What good is aim if you

never pull the trigger?

•

Are you willing to fight

for your dream?

(You have to!!!)

If you don't have a dream,

how are you going to make

a dream come true?

— *Oscar Hammerstein*

Are you known by

the promises you

don't keep?

Have you noticed

that 99 percent of the

things you worry about

don't ever happen?

Do you still believe that
anything is possible?
Or, have you come
to know better?

•

Are you going backwards
about going forward?

If you had to wear a T-shirt
printed with a message of
no more than eight words,
most accurately describing
your outlook on life, what
would your T-shirt say?

Do you question your goals by asking, "Does this particular goal help me move toward my ultimate purpose in life?"

If you don't know where
you are going, how can
you expect to get there?

Are you a winner
or a whiner?

•

Are you making dust
or eating dust?
— *Bill Grant*

Do you remember the
things you were worrying
about a year ago? How did
they work out? Didn't you
waste a lot of fruitless
energy on account of most
of them? Didn't most of
them turn out to be all
right after all?
— *Dale Carnegie*

Are you on the path of

something absolutely

marvelous or something

absolutely mediocre?

What use is running

if you are on the

wrong road?

Does failure discourage
you or make you even
more determined?

•

Are you already
disappointed with
the future?

Which is bigger? How
much you do or how
much you get done?

Is it a long way from your

words to your deeds?

Have you been

ignoring the still,

small voice inside of you?

What is it saying?

How old is your attitude?

•

Do you believe your

doubts and doubt your

beliefs?

A S K . . .

Do you judge each

day not by the harvest,

but by the seeds

you plant?

Are you making a

cemetery out of your

life by burying your

talents and gifts?

Will people say this about your life: "He did nothing in particular, and he did it very well"?

Has failure gone

to your head?

•

Are you always ready to

live, but never living?

What is your life mission?

Is it written? Are you

moving toward that life

mission or away from it?

If time and money

were no problem,

what would

you dream?

What far-reaching effects

could be set in motion by

recognizing the purpose

God has for your life and

making a real commitment

to begin to work toward

that purpose today?

Are you becoming

ordinary?

•

Does the path you're on

capture your heart?

ASK...

Do you meet the

problems and

opportunities in your

life with a decision?

Is your fear of loss

much greater than

your desire for gain?

Are you still growing?

Or just growing older?

Do you think that you
can lead a successful
sinful life?

•

How would you feel
if you didn't accomplish
your goals?

ASK...

The last time someone

asked, "What's new?"

what was your answer?

How much have the

fears and worries

that never happened

cost you?

Are you deliberately

planning to be less

than you are capable

of being?

Are you thinking of

security or opportunity?

•

What's the best use of

your time right now?

If you had the power

to do anything,

how would you

decide what to do?

Did you know to succeed

beyond your wildest

dreams, you'll have to

have some wild dreams?

If you could become

famous for one thing

in your life, what would

it be?

Ask...

If not you, then who?

If not now, then when?

— *Hillell*

•

Do you know where

you are going?

Ask yourself,

"If I didn't take action

now, what would this

ultimately cost me?"

Do you have

a bright future?

Yes? No? Why?

Are you willing to

give up what you have

in order to become

what you are not yet?

ASK...

Are you traveling, or are

you going somewhere?

•

What's most important

to you in life?

Optimism is related

to faith; pessimism

is related to doubt.

To which are you related?

What good is inspiration

if it's not backed up

with action?

Are you a person who

says, "My decision

is maybe — and

that's final"?

Are you content

with failure?

•

Does your reach exceed

your grasp?

Do you think more about what you ought to *do*, or what you ought to *be*?

Would the boy you

were be proud of the

man you are?

Do you know you

are destined to

be different?

Are you a fanatic?

•

Do you have opinions

or convictions?

What progress are

you standing in

the way of?

— *Tim Redmond*

Where did you hear

opportunity knocking?

How can you answer

that knock?

Take a look at your

natural river. Where is

your river going? Are

you riding with it? Or,

are you rowing with it?

— *Carl Frederick*

Do you build a case

against yourself?

•

Are you a person of

action or activity?

Do you try to start

with what you have

or what you

don't have?

What is one character trait

you know you display no

matter what circumstances

you are facing?

Do you know what you

set your heart on

determines how you

spend your life?

If you were not you, then

who would you be?

•

Are you a "how" thinker

or an "if" thinker?

Do you say, "I must do something," or do you say, "Something must be done"?

Do you still see yourself

the way you were when

you were age 15? 25? 35?

45? 55? 65? 75? 85? 95?

ASK...

Do you say,

"Let's find a way" or

"There is no way"?

ASK...

What is your most

prevailing thought?

•

Why don't you do what

you know you should do?

What is one decision

you would make if you

knew it would not fail?

If you were to look your

name up in the

World Book Encyclopedia,

what would it say?

When are you going

to do something new

and different?

What can you do to make
better use of your time?

•

What impossible thing
are you believing and
planning for?

ASK...

Do you say, "There should

be a better way to do it,"

or "That's the way it's

always been done"?

What would a truly

creative person do

in your situation?

Do you have a strong

will or a strong won't.

Are you making a living

or a life?

•

Who (what) are you

becoming now?

Have you found that

the place to be happy

is here, and the time to

be happy is now?

If you don't enjoy

what you have,

how could you be

happier with more?

Do you rise early

because no day is long

enough for a day's work?

If you aren't going all the

way, why go at all?

•

Do you accept miracles?

Forget your past.

Who are you now?

Who have you decided

to become?

Are you trying to

make something *for*

yourself or something

of yourself?

ASK...

After a failure

or mistake, do you give

up or get up?

Are you steering

or drifting?

•

Are you ice to truth and

fire to falsehood?

Now that it's behind

you, what did you

do yesterday that you're

proud of today?

Are you a pessimist

about the future

and an optimist

about the past?

Who of you by worrying

can add a single hour

to his life?

— *Jesus*

Napoleon is quoted
as saying: "'Impossible'
is a word found only in
the dictionary of fools."
What words are found
in *your* dictionary?

Looking
Outward

Which would you rather

have — a bouquet

of flowers or a packet

of seeds?

— *Laurie Beth Jones*

Do you tackle

problems bigger

than you?

"Who said it?"

(An important question

to ask of everything

you believe.)

Are you motivated by

what you really want

out of life, or are you

mass-motivated?

—*Earl Nightingale*

What is a fruit on the
negative-thinkers' tree?

•

If revenge is sweet,
why does it leave such
a bitter taste?

Is fear causing you

to run from something

that isn't after you?

Do you take time

you would spend with

a friend and give it

to a critic?

ASK...

Where else can you

look for answers

and ideas?

ASK...

Are you ready for your
opportunity when
it comes?

•

Do you leave others better
than you found them?

Both enthusiasm
and pessimism are
contagious. Which
one do you spread?

If someone were to pay you ten dollars for every kind word you ever spoke and collect five dollars for every unkind word, would you be rich or poor?

Are you a creature

of circumstance or a

creator of circumstance?

Does adversity shatter or

shape your life?

•

Is you favorite letter "I"?

ASK...

What would happen if you changed the words you spoke about your biggest problem? Your biggest opportunity?

Are you striking

at the branches

of your problems

or at the root?

ASK...

Are you spending your

life trying to answer

a question

nobody's asking?

Ten years from today,
what will you wish
you had done now?

•

Have you found that what
you focus on determines
how you feel?

This is the test of your life:

How much is there left

in you after you have

lost everything outside

of yourself?

— *Orison Marden*

Do you go

where opportunity

is or where opportunity

is going?

What "opportunities"
are currently before you
(or what activities are
you presently involved in)
that might really
be distractions?

When is the last time
you did a random
act of kindness?

•

Do you make others feel
bigger or smaller when
they're around you?

Every once in a while ask

yourself the question,

"If money weren't a

consideration, what

would I be doing?"

If you were another

person, would you like

to be a friend of yourself?

Did you see difficulties

in every opportunity

or opportunities in

every difficulty?

Do you go through
a problem, or try
to go around it and
never get past it?

•

Does something have
to happen in order for
you to feel good?

Do you focus on

what you don't

or what you do

want to happen?

What could you

accomplish if you

were absolutely focused

on what you want

most in life?

What will you have

to go through to

get where you

want to be?

Are you too proud
to ask for help?

•

If you try to be like
him (or her), who
will be like you?

Are you controlled by

your thoughts, or are you

controlling your thoughts?

—*Raymond Holliwell*

How can you get from

here to wherever it

is you want to be?

Do you look at the

horizon and see an

opportunity, or do you

look into the distance

and fear a problem?

Where should your

focus be?

•

What walls are you

building right now?

Whom do you

usually blame

when little or big

things go wrong?

How many people of

great potential have

you known? Where on

earth did they all go?

When confronted with a
Goliath-sized problem,
which way do you
respond: "He's too big
to hit," or, like David,
"He's too big to miss"?

What advice do you
give others that you
need to follow?

•

Do you ask more of
yourself than others do?

Do you say, "I'm good,

but not as good as I ought

to be," or do you say,

"I'm not as bad as a lot

of other people"?

What resources

and solutions are

right in front of you?

How do you act when

the pressure is on?

Can others trust you?

•

Are you running from

something or to

something?

What one thing should

you eliminate from your

life because it holds you

back from reaching

your full potential?

Do you admit,

"I was wrong,"

or do you say,

"It wasn't my fault"?

ASK...

When a problem strikes,

do you ask, "Why me?"

or "What can I learn

from this?"

ASK...

Who's creating your world?

•

Whom do you need

to forgive?

There's a force that

shapes (dominates)

your life.

What is it?

What outside influences

are causing you

to be better

or worse?

What good thing have you

previously committed

yourself to do that you

have quit doing?

Do you say, "If we can"

or "How can we?"

•

Are you blending in

or standing out?

How many people

have you made

homesick to

know God?

What is one thing you

can do for someone

else who has no

opportunity to repay you?

If the future generations

were dependent on you for

spiritual knowledge, how

much would they receive?

How many happy, selfish

people do you know?

•

How many successful

complainers do you know?

How many people

do you know became

successful at

something they hate?

If you were arrested

for being kind, would

there be enough evidence

to convict you?

ASK...

Why should people

do business with

you instead of

your competitors?

Do you make friends

before you need them?

•

Are you known as a

solution or a problem?

What task do you

most frequently put

off until tomorrow that

you should do today?

Do your friends, family,

and business associates

increase your dreams or

decrease your vision?

Do you live by the Golden

Rule today so you won't

have to apologize for

your actions tomorrow?

Are you keeping in step
with the crowd or in
step with yourself?

•

What are you really
aiming at?

When it comes to doing

things for others, are you

one of those who will

stop at nothing?

When confronted

withan obstacle,

do you become

bitter or better?

ASK...

Do you jump at

opportunities as

quickly as you jump

at conclusions?

What kind of world
would this be if everyone
was just like you?

•

When things go wrong,
do you go with them?

Did you today,

in any way, make the

world a better place

in which to live?

Are you more likely

to have an important

goal or to lack one?

Do you allow

a past circumstance

to limit today's

happiness?

If not now,

then when should

you do it?

ASK...

Do you do

odd things

to get even?

Do you anticipate

trouble and worry

about what may

never happen?

Looking
Upward

Do you put a question

mark where God has

put a period?

Do you spend the first six days of each week sowing wild oats, then go to church on Sunday and pray for a crop failure?

— *Fred Allen*

Does God seem far away?

If so, guess who moved!

•

How regularly do you

communicate with God?

Do you say "Our Father"

on Sunday and then

act like an orphan the

rest of the week?

In your prayers how

often do you say,

"And now, God, what

can I do for You?"

Can you think of
anything greater than
knowing you are in the
middle of God's will?

Are you with Him

or them?

●

Why worry when

you can pray?

Do you say:

"Good morning, Lord!"

or "Oh, no, Lord,

it's morning"?

Are you putting

out fires that

God started?

Are you willing to do what God says (or what is right) even if it means standing alone?

Hasn't God been

good to you?

•

How much of you

does God have?

If you have God's

promise for something,

isn't that enough?

What is the first,

small step you can

take to get moving?

Do you say "thank you"

to God before you ask

for something, or only

after you get it?

Are you thankful?

•

What do you believe in the

depths of your being?

Did you know that

God can give you

hindsight in advance?

Do you have a

passionate commitment

to God's plan for

your life?

Do you believe that you

were destined to be doing

what you are doing?

Why or why not?

Do you see God

everywhere or nowhere?

•

What cause are you

living for?

Who asks a king

for a penny? Why

ask God only for

something trifling?

Did you know that what

you believe is the force

that determines what you

attempt or fail to attempt

to accomplish in your life?

ASK...

Is the only time you

do any deep praying

when you find yourself

in a hole?

What puts meaning

in your life?

•

What is between

you and God?

Do you give up control

of your life to something

other than faith?

When God tells you

to do something,

do you talk back?

•

Do you risk enough to

exercise your faith in God?

The Lord is on my side;

I will not fear: what

can man do unto me?

(Psalm 118:6)

What force is more

powerful than love?

•

Is God your hope

or your excuse?

How often do you

ask God, "What are

You up to today?

Can I be a part of it?"

God has promised to be with you each step of the way (Joshua 1:9). What more can you ask for?

ASK . . .

If God so arrays the
grass of the field, which is
alive today and tomorrow
is thrown into the furnace,
will He not much more
do so for you, men
of little faith?
— *Jesus*

Is God finished

with you yet?

•

Is there anything too

hard for the Lord?

If everyone in the United

States of America were on

your level of spirituality,

would there be a revival

in the land?

The Lord is the strength

of your life; of whom

then shall you be afraid?

— Psalm 27:1

ASK...

Do you take

things for granted

or with gratitude?

Are you willing to preach
what you practice?

•

Do you reserve your
best time for communion
with God?

ASK...

What is more

miserable than being

out of God's will?

ASK...

What does God

think about

your future?

ASK...

And if you hardhearted,
sinful men know how to
give good gifts to your
children, won't your
Father in Heaven even
more certainly give
good gifts to those
who ask Him for them?
— *Jesus*

Are you waiting on God,

or is He waiting on you?

•

Is Heaven only a complaint

counter for you?

ASK...

How can the Lord guide

you if you haven't made

up your mind which way

you really want to go?

If Christ is the way,
why waste time traveling
some other path?

•

And how does a man
benefit if he gains the
whole world and loses
his soul in the process?
— *Jesus*

ASK...

When you die,

why should God let

you into Heaven?

About the Author

John Mason, best selling author and speaker, is on a mission to attack mediocrity. He speaks to the gifts and callings in people's lives, drawing out their greatest potential. He illuminates purpose and direction in others and gives them the Word to launch out.

He is the best selling author of: *An Enemy Called Average, You're Born an Original — Don't Die a Copy,* and *Let Go of Whatever Makes You Stop.* Each book is written and titled to fan the reader's potential into a blaze!

John is a popular and nationally recognized speaker at churches, conventions, and retreats, but radio is also one of John's avenues for sharing this message. His captivating radio spots called "Wait-A-Minute" are aired daily on over 400 stations across the United States. These spots are based on short excerpts from his books. Listeners have been changed by these bite-size truths for daily living.

Foremost, he is a remarkable husband and father. He, his wife Linda, and their four children, Michelle, Greg, Michael, and David, reside in Tulsa, Oklahoma.

John Mason welcomes the opportunity to speak to your church, at conferences or retreats, or to men's, women's, and youth groups. For more information about meetings, you may write or call:

John Mason
Insight International
P. O. Box 54996
Tulsa, Oklahoma 74155
918-493-1718
(fax) 918-493-2219

Additional copies of this and
the following titles by John Mason
are available from your local bookstore.

An Enemy Called Average

*Don't Wait for Your Ship to Come In —
Swim Out to Meet It*

Momentum Builders

Tulsa, Oklahoma